IN ·1776·

BY

Jean Marzollo

ILLUSTRATED BY

Steve Björkman

SCHOLASTIC
HARDCOVER

SCHOLASTIC INC.

New York

For Bud Spodek, Professor of Early Childhood Education at the University of Illinois at Urbana-Champaign, who persuasively argues that young children can understand important historical stories even before they fully understand the concept of history.

— Jean Marzollo

To the kids at Mariner's Christian School.
— Steve Björkman

Library of Congress Cataloging-in-Publication Data

Marzollo, Jean.
    IN 1776 / by Jean Marzollo; illustrated by Steve Björkman.
        p.   cm.
    Summary: Rhyming text and illustrations describe how the colonists declared their independence from Great Britain in 1776.
    ISBN 0-590-46973-8
    1. United States — History — Revolution, 1775–1783 — Juvenile literature.
    [1. United States — History — Revolution, 1775–1783.]
    I. Björkman, Steve, ill. II. Title.
    E208.M355   1993
    973.3 — dc20   92–29508
                                                                    CIP
                                                                    AC

12 11 10 9 8 7 6 5 4 3 2 1   3 4 5 6 7 8/9

Printed in the U.S.A.   37

First Scholastic printing, April 1994

The illustrations in this book were painted in watercolors.

With thanks to Kate McMullan, Ru Rauch, and especially Barry O'Connell for help with the text.

Helping Children
Understand the American Revolution

The American Revolution, like all revolutions, was neither a single event nor simply caused. It took a war to establish the independence of the colonies against Britain, but that was not itself the Revolution. The Declaration of Independence marked the beginning of a movement toward democracy, an ideal and a form of government only a few small city-states had ever before attempted.

Britain, burdened by debt from half a century of war, ending with the French and Indian War (1754–1763), began in 1764 to impose taxes upon its thirteen colonies (Massachusetts, New Hampshire, Rhode Island, Connecticut, New York, Pennsylvania, New Jersey, Delaware, Maryland, Virginia, North Carolina, South Carolina, and Georgia). The colonists' slogan, "No taxation without representation," precisely expressed their resentment of King George III's imperial ways. Disagreements and tensions increased for the next decade, finally bringing armed conflict when the British Army marched on Lexington and Concord in 1775.

The Declaration of Independence in 1776 made the break between the English colonists and the English crown irrevocable. But it was only the beginning. In its famous opening, it declared "that all men are created equal," but this did not include women, Native Americans, or African Americans, although in an early draft Jefferson had called for the abolition of slavery. For African Americans to be freed from legal slavery and discrimination required a civil war, a civil rights movement a century later, and today's continuing efforts. Only in 1920, with the ratification of the 19th Amendment to the Constitution — after great organization and agitation — did women finally gain the right to vote. When we talk with children about the American Revolution, it is important not to freeze it in the past. The struggle to create a fully democratic society, as Thomas Jefferson foresaw, requires an ongoing commitment.

Barry O'Connell, Professor, English and American Studies
Amherst College; Amherst, Massachusetts

In seventeen hundred and seventy-five,
A long, long time ago,
Great Britain ruled America —
There was some trouble, though.

The colonists were angry
Because they had no say
When the British king gave orders
Three thousand miles away.

The king said, "Pay more taxes!"
Americans said, "No!"
Some even told the British,
"It's time for you to go."

The British marched from Boston;
The farmers didn't run;
In Lexington and Concord
The fighting was begun.

In seventeen hundred and seventy-six,
Excitement filled the air;
But what the colonists needed
Was a statement to declare.

So their leaders met in Philly,
In June and in July,
They picked some men to tell the king,
"We must be free — here's why!"

The committee talked and wrote for days;
At times it wasn't fun;
Then Thomas Jefferson penned the words,
And the Declaration was done.

We hold these truths to be self-evident, that all men are created equal, that they are endowed by their Creator with certain unalienable Rights, that among these are Life, Liberty, and the pursuit of Happiness.

The Declaration of Independence
Said everyone has the right
To life, liberty, and the pursuit of happiness;
For this, men said, we'll fight!

On the Fourth of July, in seventy-six,
After a long and heated morn,
The Declaration was approved,
And the U.S.A. was born.

Americans had their statement —
Ideals worth fighting for,
A country of their very own
With liberty at the core.

American forces continued to fight;
George Washington was the chief.
Through heat and cold, they won the war . . .

And felt a great relief.

No longer ruled by a bossy king
On a distant British throne,
Americans voted in eighty-nine
For a president of their own.

Can you guess who won the vote?
Can you guess who won the day?
The winner was George Washington —
Number One in the U.S.A.

The war was over long ago;
The U.S. and Britain are now good friends.
The Declaration still guides us all;
The struggle for liberty never ends.